CELEBRATING A CENTURY AS THE GENUINE ARTICLE

The Story of OshKosh B'Gosh

CELEBRATING A CENTURY AS THE GENUINE ARTICLE

The Story of OshKosh B'Gosh 1895—1995

By James C. Naleid

GREENWICH PUBLISHING GROUP, INC.

LYME, CONNECTICUT

Printed and bound in the United States of America. No part of this publication may be reproduced or transmitted in any form or by any means, electronic or mechanical, including photocopying, recording, or any information storage and retrieval system now known or to be invented, without permission in writing from OshKosh B'Gosh, Inc., 112 Otter Avenue, Oshkosh, WI 54902, except by a reviewer who wishes to quote brief passages in connection with a review written for inclusion in a magazine, newspaper or broadcast.

Produced and published by
Greenwich Publishing Group, Inc.
Lyme, Connecticut

Design by Tom Goddard Design
Higganum, Connecticut

Separation & film assembly by
Silver Eagle Graphics, Inc.

Library of Congress Catalog Card
Number: 94-74510

ISBN: 0-944641-10-5

First Printing: March 1995

10 9 8 7 6 5 4 3 2 1

The following are current or pending trademarks of OshKosh B'Gosh, Inc.:
  B'Gosh®
  Baby B'Gosh®
  Best/Prest®
  Celebrating a Century as the
    Genuine Article™
  Genuine Kids™
  OshKosh®
  OshKosh B'Gosh®
  The Genuine Article®
  The Genuine Article Since 1895®
  Vestbak®

IZOD® is a registered trademark of
  Phillips-Van Heusen Corporation.
Levi's® is a registered trademark of
  Levi Strauss & Co.
Lee® is a registered trademark of
  The H.D. Lee Company, Inc.

Photography credits:
  p. 8 © Oshkosh Public Museum
  p. 10 middle: © Oshkosh Public
    Museum
    right: © Oshkosh Public Museum
  p. 11 middle right: © Oshkosh Public
    Museum
  p. 12 above right: © Oshkosh Public
    Museum
  p. 18 bottom: courtesy of Michael D.
    Wachtel
  p. 20 above left: courtesy of Michael
    D. Wachtel
  p. 41 courtesy of Parade Magazine
  p. 42 courtesy of Miles Kimball Co.
  p. 52 photograph taken by Oshkosh
    Northwestern. Courtesy of
    Oshkosh Public Museum

All other photographs and historical items courtesy of OshKosh B'Gosh Archives.

Photography of OshKosh B'Gosh artifacts by Timothy J. Connolly

CONTENTS

From the second floor of the Roenitz Building where OshKosh's history began to Otter Avenue, left, to New York City's Fifth Avenue, below, OshKosh B'Gosh has grown and matured. Clothing the American family for a century, the company has become a symbol of steadfast value and quality in a changeable industry and world.

INTRODUCTION

As A CITY KID, most of the men I knew went to work in factories or offices. Even so, I did know men who wore OshKosh B'Gosh bib overalls. Judging by how hard they worked, I figured a lot of hard-working men wore OshKosh B'Gosh overalls. Both of the men had the same first name, Don. One was a milkman and the other was a carpenter. This was back in the early 1950s. My buddies and I would sit on the curb early each summer morning, keeping tabs on the neighborhood. The hickory-striped bib overalls these men wore were the envy of every one of us.

Don Perkins drove a Marigold Dairy truck. He was kind of an ornery old grump, but the moms up and down the street appreciated the fact that he didn't dilly-dally on the job. They wanted the milk to be cold and the eggs fresh. Don saw to both, dependably. Every now and then he'd throw us curb-sitters a chunk of the ice that kept the milk cold. Boy, I wanted to wear a pair of those OshKosh B'Gosh bib overalls when I grew up.

Don Johnson was the best carpenter in town. My dad hired him to put an addition on our house — the biggest addition you'd ever seen. Don wore his OshKosh B'Gosh bibs with professional pride. In a small narrow pocket, attached to the side of his right leg like a built-in holster, he carried one of those foldable wooden rulers. You know, the kind that opens up and just keeps growing and growing and growing. That ruler was twice as big as I was and fit inside just one small pocket. He always carried his hammer at the ready on the other side of his bib overalls, in the loop. Don knew everything about building. He could build steps and all kinds of things. One day he showed me how he could blow through a copper tube to make a sound just like a slide trombone. Like the two Dons, someday I, too, would wear a pair of OshKosh B'Gosh bib overalls.

I did wear a pair one day, and many days after, in Berkeley, California, circa 1969. The blond-haired kids who grew up in southern California surfin' to the tunes of the Beach Boys didn't know what life really had to offer in the Midwest, but they would just about kill or pay any price for a pair of those OshKosh B'Gosh bib overalls. Twenty-six years later, my 17-year-old kid is wearing OshKosh B'Gosh bib overalls as fashionable ski wear. He, of course, does not realize that the bandana around his neck and the denim bibs came into fashion a hundred years ago. My, how things haven't changed.

Frank Grove, Howie Jenkins, Jim Clark, Bill Pollock, Sam Pickard, Earl Wyman, his son Tom and grandson Bill, along with Earl's son-in-law Fritz Hyde, his son Doug and Fritz's son-in-law Mike Wachtel span a hundred years of cotton denim, union-made workwear and an illustrious history. Together they have created a style and a reputation for quality that is as much a part of Americana as apple pie and as ice cream in the summertime.

It would be grand to gather all of these men, the genealogy of the company, together in the boardroom at 112 Otter Avenue in Oshkosh, Wisconsin. Though Grove, Jenkins, Clark, Pollock, Pickard and Earl Wyman are gone, their contributions remain.

As OshKosh B'Gosh stands poised to begin its journey into a second century of providing the world with ruggedly fashionable work and casual wear and delightfully colorful children's clothes, we will look back to remember the road so recently traveled. This is the centennial story about common threads in an American dream.

James C. Naleid
March, 1995

Headlight

SOUVENIR EDITION

OSHKOSH, WIS.

Sights and Scenes ALONG

THE NORTHWESTERN LINE.

CHICAGO, ILL.

CHAPTER ONE

RUGGED-WEAR, RAILROADS AND UNOFFICIAL UNIFORMS

IN PURSUIT OF the new prosperity, hard-working immigrants built the city of Oshkosh, Wisconsin, along the banks of the Fox River between Lake Butte des Mortes and the western shore of Lake Winnebago in 1853. Many of the men and women who first came there probably knew one another and shared common dreams. Though it was a beautiful spot, life was hard and the comforts few.

One of the city's early industries, incorporated in July 1895, was the Grove Manufacturing Company, which made tough overalls for working men. There were four original partners of the company — Frank E. Grove, J. Howard Jenkins, James Clark and George M. Jones — each of whom invested $6,250 to capitalize the company. As the company was named after Grove, it appears as though the

idea to start the company was his, but he clearly needed the working capital, and perhaps the management skills, his partners provided.

Just one year after the company was established, two of the partners, Jenkins and Clark, bought the business from Grove. (Unable to come up with his $6,250 investment, Jones's shares were canceled by the end of 1895 and his involvement with the company ended.) Proud community citizens, Jenkins and Clark changed the company name to Oshkosh Clothing Manufacturing Company on December 22, 1896. The reasons why Grove sold out to his partners have been lost to history. Besides old newspaper clippings noting his death in 1920, not much is known about Grove or his wife, Lillian, who suffered an early death in 1890, well before Grove Manufacturing came into existence.

When Jenkins and Clark agreed to purchase the business, it was housed on the second floor of the Roenitz Building over on Commerce Street. Ten employees came with the deal. Jenkins and Clark had ambitious plans and wasted little time before pursuing them. Six years after acquiring the company, they moved to Otter Avenue into

The grueling physical labor required to build and run the railroads that tamed the West created a market for OshKosh's unusually durable clothing, and the company's early success can be traced, in large part, to the proliferation of railroads. The Northwestern railroad proudly promoted the city of Oshkosh as one of its destinations in the souvenir, left. The photograph, above, shows employees responsible for two major steps in the manufacturing process: a row of women at their sewing machines in the foreground and the fabric cutters at their tables in the background.

the building that is still the corporate headquarters today.

Jenkins, who took the titles of president and treasurer, had many outside business interests which absorbed much of his time and energy. He was involved in banking, insurance and the Mexican Development and Construction Corporation, of which he was president. (Jenkins was also an accomplished musician and is said to have played a part in the writing of the famous Civil War ditty, "John Brown's Body.") James Clark, who had immigrated to the United States from England, was vice president and secretary. Regardless of their respective titles, Clark was the one who oversaw the day-to-day operations of the company and managed the business. Under Clark's careful guidance in those early years, Oshkosh Clothing Manufacturing began to take on its unique flavor. A prime ingredient was its special connection with American laborers and farmers.

Particularly along the western shore of Lake Michigan, where Wisconsin's industrial base flourished, the political persuasion of the era had direct ties to socialist ideology. As the nation's industrial fire swept westward along the shores of the Great Lakes, workers' unions were formed and consequently played a meaningful role in providing equitable treatment for the immigrants who were attracted to the new world's opportunities. In keeping with such trends, Jenkins and Clark invited the United Garment Workers of America on board and issued a charter to Local Chapter 126. The "Union Made" label would, in time, become an important ingredient in their marketing scheme.

The bib overalls from the Oshkosh Manufacturing Company provided farmers, railroad men and industrial workers with more convenience than a leather apron. Suspenders were attached securely, and stress

Owners Howard Jenkins and James Clark created the "J & C" brand to differentiate their rugged overalls from those of lower quality made by competitors.

In step with the times politically and otherwise, Jenkins, left, and Clark, right, understood the union movement sweeping the Great Lakes region and invited the garment workers union on board as one of their first acts when they acquired the company. Winning the business of railroad workers was an important part of their marketing strategy. Wherever the railroads went, so went retailers who sold the company's products.

points were reinforced in the sturdy over-garment designed to protect a typical pair of cotton sewn work pants. As a matter of fact, in later years one Iowa retailer suggested the overalls were "tough as a mule's hide."

To differentiate their work wear from others, the "J & C" brand name was adopted and woven into the stripe of the denim in some of their garments. This satisfied the egos of the new owners and separated their clothing from that which was manufactured by others. Their business strategy was simple — make the best doggone workwear to be found. They knew the customer they wanted to serve; he worked the rivers and the big lakes, plowed the land and rode the long gray ribbon of steel rails across the country.

As the company grew and prospered, it offered opportunities for many a long and satisfying career. When Anna Knaak came looking for work at the Oshkosh Manufacturing Company in 1905, she had no idea her experience there would span nearly six decades. Anna started work as an inspector for four dollars a week, and her pride and sense of loyalty were noticed early on. The inspection station was not to be her "home" for long. Soon, she joined the sewers, known for their dexterity and skill. Years later, while addressing fellow employees, Anna proclaimed, "I never woke up any morning that I wasn't happy to come to work." Loving her job helped get her out of bed for 58 years without one day of tardiness to tarnish her impeccable work record.

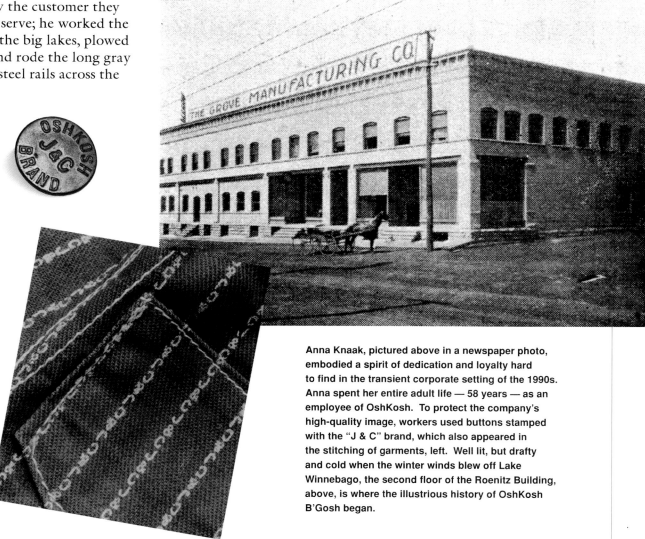

Anna Knaak, pictured above in a newspaper photo, embodied a spirit of dedication and loyalty hard to find in the transient corporate setting of the 1990s. Anna spent her entire adult life — 58 years — as an employee of OshKosh. To protect the company's high-quality image, workers used buttons stamped with the "J & C" brand, which also appeared in the stitching of garments, left. Well lit, but drafty and cold when the winter winds blew off Lake Winnebago, the second floor of the Roenitz Building, above, is where the illustrious history of OshKosh B'Gosh began.

Son of a dry goods merchant in Ford County, Illinois, William Pollock, top, arrived at the Oshkosh Clothing Manufacturing Company when he was 38. He changed the company's name to the Oshkosh Overall Company and introduced OshKosh B'Gosh, which would become the world's most famous brand name in quality work and children's wear. When Pollock arrived in 1910, there were just 24 employees producing the company's products.

CHAPTER TWO

THE OSHKOSH B'GOSH BRAND IS BORN

T WENTY-FOUR employees manned the pattern-cutting and sewing tables in 1910, when a dapper, red-headed Chicagoan arrived on the scene. Barrel-chested and not much more than five feet tall, William Edward Pollock bought half of the company from Jenkins and Clark. It was a logical career move for Pollock. After prospering as a salesman of women's accessories and corsets, he represented Bread Winner Overalls of Burlington, Vermont, and W.M. Finck Overalls of Detroit, Michigan. It couldn't be said that he didn't know the ins and outs of the business, at least from a hard-driving salesman's point of view.

Clark remained president for the time being. Pollock's brother David bought a quarter of the business from Clark and served as vice president for several years. Without fanfare — though he later earned a reputation as a colorful manager — Pollock changed the name of the company to the Oshkosh Overall Company.

William Pollock enjoyed the theater, on or off Broadway. A friend of vaudeville and a frequent patron of the

arts, it wasn't uncommon for Pollock to take in a show when visiting Chicago or other big cities. As lore has it, OshKosh B'Gosh was not born of creative marketing genius, but rather was something Pollock heard uttered by a member of the cast during a night at the theater. He liked the sound of it — catchy, trendy. The brand would be known as OshKosh B'Gosh from then on. Little did he realize the fanciful phrase "OshKosh B'Gosh" would one day be spoken throughout the world to refer

The OshKosh B'Gosh brand name would travel by rail, horse-drawn delivery van, motorized automobiles and across the backs of mules, perhaps reinforcing the claim that the company's products were as "tough as a mule's hide." Brand recognition has always been important to the company. Retailers historically have been encouraged to find innovative ways of promoting the brand.

The origin of the company's use of Uncle Sam in various promotions has been lost to time, but many examples are housed in the company's archives today. An undated photograph of Otter Avenue shows the company's headquarters when trolley tracks ran down the street.

to much more than blue denim or hickory-striped overalls.

However, there's another version, according to a local journalist who reported it in a daily newspaper in 1928. "One day Mr. Pollock was sitting at a lunch counter in a small town in Iowa when he noticed an advertisement for a safety razor that depicted Uncle Sam shaving. As he shaved, Uncle Sam said, 'They come off slick as a whistle b'gosh.' It was then that Mr. Pollock thought, 'Why not Oshkosh B'Gosh?'" Though the popular vaudeville version of the story is more glamorous, there's an equal chance that the lunch-counter version is the truth and was later embellished for the sake of color.

William E. Pollock grew his investment the old-fashioned way — with a combina-

tion of hard work and calculated risks. Most knew him as a gifted and determined entrepreneur with a management style all his own. The industrial age brought with it new machines, new concepts and more efficient means to produce goods of all kinds. Seven years after buying ownership in the company, Pollock decided the chance he took would pay more handsomely if he expanded the old storefront on Otter Avenue and updated its operations. He initiated a major construction and remodeling project in 1917, as United States involvement in World War I heightened. Pollock's timing could not have been better.

Following World War I, the Oshkosh Overall Company flourished during the economic boom of the Roaring Twenties. Towards the decade's end, Pollock made a decision that

OSHKOSH B'GOSH

UNION MADE OVERALLS

**The Work Clothes for Dad
The Play Clothes for Sonny**

Dad is here shown wearing the "Allover" Overall. It covers the body amply yet leaves the arms perfectly free. The ideal overall for the farm. Made strong, roomy, comfortable, of heavy durable Eastern denim. Sonny is wearing a pair of regular overalls, of the same heavy material and made just as strong and durable as dad's. A new pair of either without cost if the first pair is not satisfactory.

OSHKOSH OVERALL CO.   OSHKOSH, WIS.

*They Must Make Good
Or We Will*

suggests foresight on his part. Early in 1929, the company was restructured, and the Oshkosh Overall Company incorporated under the laws of the state of Delaware, a common practice for American companies because of that state's favorable tax laws and business regulations. While Mr. Pollock maintained his majority stake in the company, the decision was made to raise capital through a preferred and common stock offering.

A stock offering circular of March 1929 noted that 10,000 active customers had ordered Oshkosh Overall products. With the exception of 1920, which was a difficult year following the close of World War I, the company reported profits every year, with peak revenues of $1,900,000 in 1928. The offering memorandum makes it clear that management ran a frugal,

A 1919 company advertisement, left, had a "like father, like son" theme which encouraged multiple purchases of overalls. The ad contained the company's satisfaction guarantee — "They must make good or we will." In 1917, workers paraded in front of the Otter Avenue building, above, as part of President Woodrow Wilson's "Preparedness Campaign," that was introduced in January 1916 to increase public awareness of the need to prepare for World War I.

tight-fisted operation, as current cash assets listed by the company outnumbered liabilities by a margin of nearly six to one. Nonetheless, in the five years preceding the new stock offering, annual revenues had grown at a snail's pace of just two percent a year. During that period, the company's sales growth had slowed considerably while the number of employees had burgeoned from the 24 Pollock inherited when he took control to several hundred at the time of the stock offering.

Once again, Pollock's timing was right on the money.

The stock markets were climbing to new highs just as the offering was made, and Pollock sold a large percentage of his ownership at the high point. It was only a matter of months following the equity offering that the stock market in the United States took the biggest fall ever, the crash of 1929 that ushered in the Great Depression. Chaos within the financial markets ruined many families and brought companies of all sorts to their knees. The Oshkosh Overall Company, however, survived.

Miriam M. Knaggs, the granddaughter-in-law of one of the city of Oshkosh's first settlers, remembers the depression. She was hired in 1929 for

a "temporary" position that lasted 44 years, as her skills, accuracy and attention to detail were recognized by her managers and workmates. The Great Depression left Miriam and her fellow workers with one primary concern: keeping their jobs. They took nothing for granted and attended to the company's needs without reservation and consequently rode out the difficult early years of the 1930s.

With eyes twinkling from the glee of vivid recollections, Miriam speaks of Pollock with fondness. He was a kind man, hot-tempered at times but always fair. She remembers how Pollock could be heard

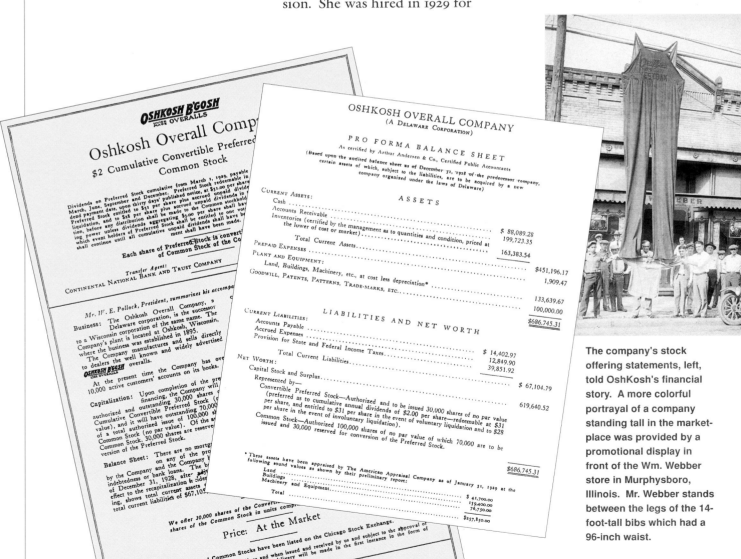

The company's stock offering statements, left, told OshKosh's financial story. A more colorful portrayal of a company standing tall in the marketplace was provided by a promotional display in front of the Wm. Webber store in Murphysboro, Illinois. Mr. Webber stands between the legs of the 14-foot-tall bibs which had a 96-inch waist.

leaving his office and taking the circuitous route through and around the first floor of the finishing room and packing rooms at 112 Otter Avenue, making his way to the front administrative offices. Many of the 450-odd employees learned to gauge his demeanor well before his arrival, based upon the velocity of his gait as he walked or marched the wooden floors.

Pollock lived to be nearly 90 years old, and his love for the city of Oshkosh manifested itself many times over. His employees' regard for him must have been high, as it was the United Garment Workers Local 126 that sponsored his retirement party, when he was honored for his years of ownership at a gala farewell dinner at the Athearn Hotel, "The Astor of Oshkosh."

FAREWELL DINNER

in honor of

W. E. POLLOCK

by

U. G. W. of A.
Local 126

Saturday Eve., December 22
Nineteen Hundred Thirty-four

ATHEARN HOTEL

Workers gather in front of the Otter Avenue building on a winter day sporting the fashions of the times, left. Advertisements in magazines, above left, and painted on the sides of buildings in towns large and small, below, brought awareness of the company's name and its products. By the time Pollock's retirement dinner was held, above, the company was already in the hands of Earl Wyman, who would lead it for the next generation.

This storefront in Marshfield, Wisconsin, in 1939, shows a variety of OshKosh products along with posters announcing a visit by radio personality Johnnie "OshKosh B'Gosh" Olson. A poster, top, offered clickers to customers. The large paperclip, left, was another of the many promotional items given to retailers.

CHAPTER THREE

WHO IS THIS WYMAN FELLA?

BUY LOW, SELL HIGH." That's what smart investors will tell you. It's an axiom that Pollock followed brilliantly when he made the 1929 stock offering. By the time he was ready to find a buyer for the company five years later in the midst of the Great Depression, "selling high" was a tougher challenge.

Nobody alive today really knows what Earl Wyman, a former bond salesman cum insurance specialist, saw in the opportunity he uncovered in 1934. For whatever reasons, he was able to convince a business friend and peer that the Oshkosh Overall Company was a good investment, and the two joined together to buy Pollock's controlling interest. At best recollection, Wyman and Sam Pickard paid $4 a share, a price they obviously considered attractive.

Sam Pickard and Earl Wyman were introduced to one another over mutual interests in Ripon, Wisconsin, 20 miles away from Oshkosh. Pickard, a reputable banker, was not a newcomer to buying and revitalizing companies. His impeccable business reputation

was built upon a foundation of integrity and the ability to assess value— and Sam Pickard looked deeper than the overall worth of the bricks and mortar when he evaluated a company. More often than not, he bet on the man. Apparently, he thought Earl Wyman was worth a substantial wager, even though Wyman had not one minute of experience in the clothing business. Outsiders might well have questioned his judgment. What, after all, did Earl Wyman and Sam Pickard know about running an overall-manufacturing company?

Wyman's experience, however, included some important facets. As a bond salesman, he understood debt. He knew a balance sheet when he saw one. Looking at most companies from the debt side of their ledger sheets, he also understood that equity, if acquired at the right price, could become a very valuable asset. It would take a few years for his assumptions to become manifest, but this 40-year-old family man, with a successful career behind him, was ready to use all of the skills he possessed to run the

Blessed with an eye for success, former Northwestern Mutual Life Insurance agent Earl Wyman envisioned big things for his newly acquired company. He would lead OshKosh to its 50th anniversary celebration and beyond.

company he and his partner now controlled. His wife would tell their children years later, "Your father is a bright man, but more important than anything else, he uses everything he's got to get the job done. He wastes nothing."

Earl Wyman and Sam Pickard were willing to put their hunch on the line, even to the point of borrowing and

The women pictured at right are using specially designed sewing machines in the "felling" process. This part of the construction of the overall involves sewing together the fully completed front piece and back piece of the garment. Sewing down the outside seam on one leg, around the inseam and back up the outside seam of the other leg, the women would use these "Union Special feed-off-the-arm" machines to combine the pieces into a single garment. A handwritten breakdown of the cost of each garment allowed the company to analyze the benefits of using new fabrics such as the chambray listed below in order #102.

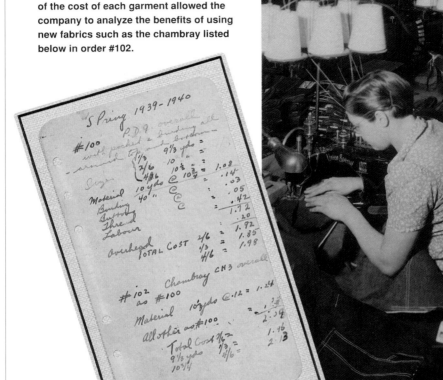

Every order was sewn by hand on foot-operated machines such as this Wilcox and Gibbs machine. This "modern" sewing equipment pounded needle and thread through the heavy denim used in the company's rugged outerwear.

collateralizing their future. They bought a company with one thing in mind; to make it better and more profitable than it had ever been. Though Pollock had undertaken a sizable renovation project early in his tenure, what Wyman and Pickard found when they actually rolled up their sleeves was a physical plant and equipment in need of serious updating. In reality, it had been close to 15 years since much attention had been given to either.

Besides those concerns, Wyman's first challenge as new chief executive was to work out a new balance of power be-

tween his management team and the garment workers' union. Over time, the union had gained an unusual degree of control over the operation. Those who knew say Pollock's son Ken did not like the control and influence the union held over the company. Wyman found out why shortly after taking the boss's chair. Organizationally, one might wonder who really made company decisions. The union controlled the shop floor, and its supervisors chose when to hire and when to fire, when to produce and when not to. Earl Wyman needed to change that,

OshKosh was building a reputation as an all-American company. Though the corporate letterhead has taken different forms, right, each design shows the pride that OshKosh B'Gosh had in its workers. The consistent use of the guarantee, "They better make good, or we will!" and the association with Uncle Sam emphasized the company's recognition of who their customers were: hard-working, patriotic citizens with respect for a hard-working product.

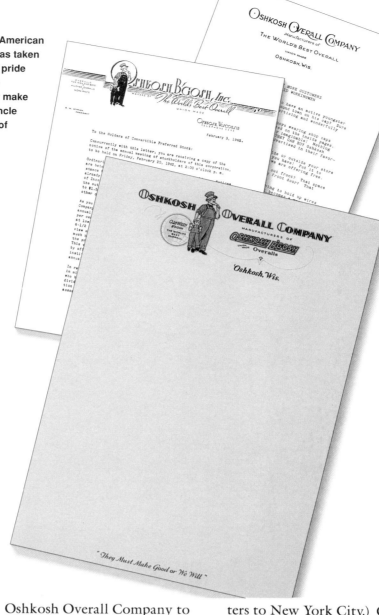

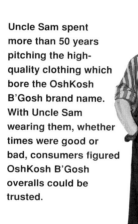

Uncle Sam spent more than 50 years pitching the high-quality clothing which bore the OshKosh B'Gosh brand name. With Uncle Sam wearing them, whether times were good or bad, consumers figured OshKosh B'Gosh overalls could be trusted.

and in the process, he became a skilled negotiator.

Wyman took control of the company. He changed things. As a student at Ripon College, he had captained many a fine basketball team to victory. At the helm of the Oshkosh Overall Company, he applied the same leadership and determination to succeed. Recognizing how valuable the brand name "OshKosh B'Gosh" had become, Wyman believed the most efficient way to protect it would be to name the company for it. The decision was made to change the name of the company from the

Oshkosh Overall Company to OshKosh B'Gosh, Inc. in February of 1937. It was this name, this brand and the people behind it that would put Oshkosh, Wisconsin, on the map, so to speak.

Wyman and his management team also knew when to look outside the company for advice. In early March 1941, the company retained the services of Kurt Salmon Associates, which at the time was a Washington, D.C.-based engineering consulting firm. (Kurt Salmon Associates, now more commonly referred to as KSA, Inc., has since relocated its headquar-

ters to New York City.) C.E. Whimack, who served under both Pollock and Wyman as vice president, worked closely with the consultants, who would ultimately save the company an estimated $26,000 a year — no small chunk of change in those days. Retaining the consultants, who made their final report to the company in December 1943, proved to be a management decision of undeniable value. The recommendations implemented led to greater productivity and efficiencies and undoubtedly signaled that Earl Wyman was clearly calling the shots. His

At the ripe old age of 50, OshKosh B'Gosh was just beginning to pick up speed, and Wyman's wish for an equally successful second 50 years would ultimately come true. The Golden Jubilee in 1946 celebrated much more than a half-century of successful business. The cover and inside spread of the Jubilee's program, below, indicate the tone of the celebration. The focus of the evening was on the contribution OshKosh B'Gosh made to American workers — not only by producing a quality product for customers to wear, but also by providing a quality company for its employees.

success at establishing control and increasing profitability was evident 12 years later, when the company celebrated its Golden Jubilee — 50 years of being in business. (World War II delayed the celebration for a full year until 1946.)

During the evening of the gala event, Lawrence Reno, then president of Local 126 of the United Garment Workers, presented Wyman with a floral arrangement and spoke before the 400 or more in attendance saying, "Our gift to you is our ability and skill to carry on and make the company better and bigger than it has ever been before."

Some might suggest such a comment was nothing more than public rhetoric on Reno's part, but in fact, he and Wyman had become good friends over the years and were often seen together at company functions more than politely enjoying one another's company. Whatever Earl

Wyman had to do when he arrived as the company's new leader, he must have done it with a firm but understanding and reasonable hand.

The night of the Jubilee brought other labor dignitaries to Oshkosh. George Haberman, a big name in Wisconsin labor who served as the president of the Wisconsin State Federation of Labor, came up from Milwaukee for the night and addressed the crowd. Turning to Wyman, he said, "Wisconsin has benefited by your organization; nothing but good has come from your establishment in 50 years. Such cooperation for the benefit of humanity is only accomplished if sound, reasonable relationships exist between management and labor. We have pointed to your organization from coast to coast as an institution where labor and management can get along if it has the will and heart to do so. We point to your company as an example of

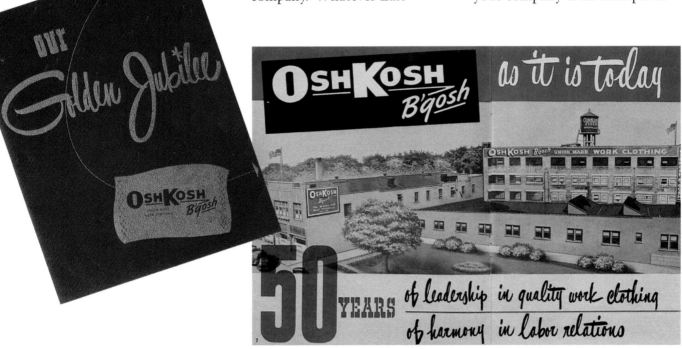

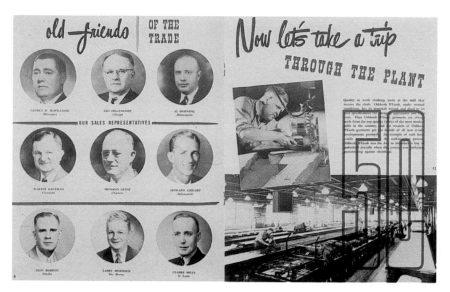

The Jubliee program demonstrated the company's appreciation of the employees who had contributed to OshKosh's success. Pictured in the program, above, were people from every part of the company's operations, many of them veterans from Pollock's days.

sound labor management — it can work if you see fit to make it work; 50 years is not to be denied." Earl Wyman smiled, the audience applauded.

Mind you, this was not a celebration in honor of Earl Wyman, but by the sound of things, it almost appeared to be. There are other facts worth noting. At the time of the Jubilee, 227 of the 450 employees had been with the firm for 10 years or less. That means they had been hired after Wyman's arrival. Sixty-five of the employees there had been working for OshKosh B'Gosh for more than 25 years. Ed Wurl and Anna Knaak survived Jenkins, Clark and Pollock to mark up more than 40 years each with the company. There's no doubt that the leadership role Wyman played contributed significantly to the opportunity and stability these employees enjoyed while working at the company.

Knowing Earl Wyman, employees and colleagues alike sensed there was more on his mind than just the present. Close associates tell of how he paused each time a hearse carrying a local farmer or railroad man passed by, knowing that the community had lost a good citizen and that the company had probably lost another loyal customer — OshKosh's customer base was shrinking. He knew the scene of the Midwest was changing and so too must the company he captained if it were to remain on top. Long before diversification of product lines actually came to be, he knew future prosperity would have to be fueled not by sales of overalls alone, but also by items that were yet to be conceived.

Above, a retailer announces that he carries the famous OshKosh B'Gosh brand of denim workwear. Who wouldn't be proud to model America's finest overall? If retailers saw fit to use an entire outside wall to advertise the OshKosh B'Gosh name, men and boys happily wore it across their chest. Because the company offered free painting of signs like this, they were commonly seen around the country — and were certainly hard to miss.

Kurt Salmon Associates, engineering and manufacturing consultants, suggested significant changes in production and manufacturing processes. Their recommendations brought not only increased efficiency and enhanced quality standards, but also better working conditions — thus increasing both customer and employee satisfaction.

CHAPTER FOUR

THE NEXT GENERATION COMES ON THE SCENE

W HILE EARL WYMAN was concentrating on strengthening the OshKosh B'Gosh name, he and his wife Naomi were raising a family. Their children, Tom and Joyce, would eventually be linked with the company. In 1941, another person appeared who would ultimately figure in the future of OshKosh B'Gosh.

As the summer of 1941 arrived, the world was boiling with political and military activity, but 14-year-old Tom Wyman was far more concerned with the promise of the months ahead. His vivacious 17-year-old sister, Joyce, was equally ready for whatever that summer would bring.

On Park Street in Oshkosh, one neighborhood friend home from college invited a fraternity brother and a couple of sidekicks from New Jersey for a visit later that summer. Charles "Fritz" Hyde just happened to be one of the three lads who drove into town in a big old Mercury convertible, complete with wide whitewall tires and huge chrome bumpers. Bound for California, the boys

stayed in Oshkosh for only a short time. Friendships had been struck, however, and though Joyce Wyman and Fritz Hyde may not have realized it, their relationship was just beginning.

Fritz Hyde and Joyce Wyman would meet again, but

not right away. Joyce planned to attend college out east, and more than likely, she and Fritz would figure out a way to see each other. They did, several times. Meanwhile, the Japanese attack on Pearl Harbor focused the country's attention on the war effort. Fritz Hyde, like

Learning the business from the bottom up helped prepare Fritz Hyde, left, for the dramatic industry changes that heralded OshKosh B'Gosh's second 50 years. Though garment design and sales strategies were to begin almost continual transition, Fritz carried the long-established tradition of quality products and sound business ethics into modern times.

OshKosh had its own role to play in the war effort and company employees showed their dedication to the troops in combat. OshKosh produced dungarees and shirts for the navy and one-piece "jungle suits" for the ground forces. The garments had the same toughness and durability that farmers and workers had counted on for years — only the fabric and colors changed.

The radio room, above, was connected to a loudspeaker system on the factory floor. It was used for company announcements and broadcasted appropriate music for 15 minutes out of every hour.

thousands of his peers, decided to join the national counterattack. Fritz signed himself up in the V7 Naval Reserve Officer Training Program, a two-year college program that prepared him to become a communications officer in the navy.

World War II temporarily kept Fritz and Joyce apart, but they stayed in touch. By the time OshKosh B'Gosh was preparing for its Jubilee Celebration, Fritz and Joyce were preparing to marry. After their wedding, Fritz took a job with a glove manufacturer in Illinois, and before long, the new Mr. and Mrs. Hyde accepted a relocation assignment to Winona, Minnesota. While Fritz's employers recognized his leadership skills, Earl Wyman was keeping an eye on his son-in-law's business career, too. Their next move, in 1948, was one Joyce had some doubts about: her father invited Fritz to join OshKosh B'Gosh. Her brother, Tom, would be finish-

ing his college courses in 1949, and as far as Earl was concerned, it was time to start thinking about the company's future in the next generation.

Fritz and Joyce enjoyed Winona during their brief stay, but Earl's invitation was enough to bring them back to Oshkosh. Joyce never really thought she would settle in her hometown, but in retrospect, she's the first to admit, "It's been a terrific place to raise my family, and we've had many great years living in this community."

As an outsider, Fritz had a lot to learn about OshKosh B'Gosh. He spent his first months writing garment-construction manuals, which his father-in-law figured would help him get to know the company's product lines inside out. After that, he learned the ropes from some of the old sales pros and eventually was given his own territory.

This advertisement, left, from *Successful Farming* publicizes one of the countless industry innovations initiated by OshKosh B'Gosh. Such innovations increased after the war as military uniforms inspired a new look for workwear. OshKosh broadened its advertising strategy and its clothing line to match the changing postwar workforce. Below, the new image included casual wear and work clothes in more modern fabrics for everyone from cab drivers to "do-it-yourselfers."

When Tom Wyman arrived a year later, diversification away from just the blue denim and hickory-striped bib overalls was well underway, and the company was doing a lot of things incorporating chino, twill and chambray cottons into the various product lines. Tom was sent south to Atlanta to visit the mills that supplied the company's raw materials. He got to know the red clay roads of Georgia and the hard-working folks who wove cotton into fabrics that his company would cut, shape and sew a union-made OshKosh B'Gosh label on one day.

Whether they fully realized it or not, the new generation of leaders had arrived. They had much to learn, but they had arrived, b'gosh.

Tom Wyman began his career at OshKosh preparing for the new era of fashionable workwear and the ever-changing demands from customers. By learning early on what it takes to supply the materials for new fashions, Tom was able to steer the company through decades of change.

OshKosh was always ready to help the retailers who were the sole distribution system of OshKosh products. The numerous locations in this article from OshKosh's magazine, *Builder-Upper*, show how the reputation for quality of the OshKosh B'Gosh brand name was moving across the country.

OshKosh ads and labels proudly linked the company's products with its working people — a connection that was established at the very beginning of its history.

CHAPTER FIVE

BEYOND BLUE DENIM AND HICKORY STRIPES

THROUGHOUT the forties, the OshKosh B'Gosh brand name became part of the Midwestern vocabulary, helped by an aggressive marketing and advertising campaign that plastered it on the sides of barns, silos and general stores and along the rural byways and highways throughout the farmbelt. Dealers were encouraged to order signs for their storefronts. From Tucumcari, New Mexico, to Clinton, Minnesota, retailers responded to a piece in the OshKosh B'Gosh newsletter, *Builder Upper*, that advised, "Every active, growing OshKosh B'Gosh dealer should jump at the opportunity to get these large steel enameled road signs FREE." The company promised the goods — all the dealer had to do was provide the space. These weren't cheap signs, by the way. According to the marketing pitch, "These colorful 32 x 46 inch metal signs are framed in wood — if you were to order five or ten of them yourself, they would cost you more than $10.00 each!"

The voice of OshKosh B'Gosh was heard across the land in those years. It boomed out from the geographical center of North America, near Smoky Lake in North Dakota, over radio station WDAY out of Fargo, to Chicago, where the renowned call letters of WLS broadcast the advertising message of the day. WDKA in Pittsburgh and WBT in Charlotte carried the slogans of everyday workwear to the eastern seaboard. Belk's Department Store in Charlotte, Korrick's in Phoenix, Goldsmith's in Memphis and eventually Meier & Frank Company in Portland, Fishers in Tacoma and Smith's in Oakland were among the many major retailers from one side of the country to the other who sold OshKosh B'Gosh goods to their customers before the decade came to a close.

THE FAMOUS STAR OF STAGE, SCREEN AND RADIO

ANDY DEVINE

NEW RADIO SPOTS TELLS YOU AND YOUR CUSTOMERS ABOUT

OSHKOSH B'gosh

Andy Devine was a spokesman for OshKosh B'Gosh for a number of years, and recordings of his radio spots were sent to retailers who could run them on local radio, play them in stores or take them home. This is the cover of an old 45 rpm recording, the popular format in those days.

These 50-foot-long marking tables, top, were used to lay out, mark and cut multiple bolts of denim at the same time, using heavy cutting machines like the one pictured at left. Bib straps, above, await seamstresses who will sew them in place.

While the company was growing in size and reputation, Tom Wyman and Fritz Hyde were busy learning the ropes. Tom had grown up around the place and worked there as a teenager and college student, but his new connection with the company lent greater urgency to the lessons he had to learn.

Tom spent the decade working the manufacturing end of the business, learning the angles while developing management skills he would need later on. He watched and listened as his father and others shared their secrets and understanding of how the business was run. He combined his growing knowledge of the process with the lessons his father shared about buying the right fabric at the right price.

BIG COLORFUL BANDANA **FREE !** YOURS JUST FOR LOOKING!

The OshKosh B'Gosh red bandana was one of the company's most popular promotions. Tens of thousands of these trademark bandanas were given away to customers: men would use them to wipe their brows or protect their necks; women to cover their heads; teenagers to stuff in a back pocket. All would help the company advertise one of the most famous brands in the world.

Clarence Bursack, the company's "bean counter," kept track of costs. He knew what it meant to save a penny where needed and taught Tom what he knew.

These were years of change, which brought an interest in new fabrics and new weights of denim. Tom brought an openness to new possibilities, an attitude that came at the right time. Some resisted the gradual move away from the familiar. They'd say, "It can't be done!" It could, it had to and Tom, never losing sight of his father's concern for the future, knew it.

Change had already become a matter of survival then. OshKosh B'Gosh faced a country of changing lifestyles and changing tastes in the years following the war. From the fields to the factories, folks demanded a little pizazz on their backs, clothes that expressed the postwar "can-do" attitude. Working America was in migration. All across the continental United States, a movement from the farm to the city and suburb was underway.

In 1951, OshKosh B'Gosh launched a promotion to catch up with the folks who were leaving the farms — and those who had never been there. The campaign handed out red bandanas to everyone who stopped by the local merchant's store to examine an OshKosh B'Gosh garment.

Men, women and children could have the privilege of becoming an advertisement by wearing the free bandana with its trademark OshKosh B'Gosh triangle. Young boys could stuff them into the back pockets of their sturdy OshKosh B'Gosh BRONKS, blue jeans built tough but with a colorful hip pocket ticket and embossed genuine leather label that the boys really went for. Women and girls found the bandanas ideally suited for use as a head scarf, or as they say in the old country, babushka.

Work pants and shirts for men, in particular, took on a more tailored neatness. The laborer of the 1950s wanted to go to work in the same fashion he fought a war — uniformed, starting the day crisp and sharp as a tack. Military-issue khaki was a natural extension of what the war experience brought home in fashion as well.

Along with rock 'n roll and blue suede shoes came the ever-popular blue jeans, worn by anyone who knew what being hip was all about. Of course, guys in the know rolled a pretty decent size cuff on each pant leg, just enough to allow one's socks — preferably white ones — to be seen.

Suddenly, the durable OshKosh B'Gosh denims were being worn by a whole new generation of Americans. Thanks to the changing needs and desires of fashion-conscious consumers, this company was ready to dress the whole family, even putting their western style BRONKS on young men and boys and BRONKETTES on the girls!

Proud to have worn crisp, neatly tailored military uniforms, homebound World War II veterans reentered the workforce wanting clothing with the same proud, crisp look, top. Blue denim overalls gave way to updated styling in khaki and chino cotton fabrics that could be worn at work, at home or even while fishing, as the ad above from the 1940s suggests. The rugged BRONKS worn by the models in an ad, right, promoted "smart cowboy styling" as part of a western look that was popular at the time.

Analyzing sales trends, management learned that sportswear was rapidly becoming a larger segment of the business. Different processes were needed. Folks other than the typical loyalists — the farm and train people — were beginning to buy OshKosh B'Gosh products. The swing in the fashion pendulum meant new growth for the company — a reality every successful business manager confronts at some point in time. According to the business books, growth is good, growth is necessary, and one must manage for growth because without it, you're apt to shrivel up and fade away.

Earl Wyman didn't like the word "fade." He insisted on fabric that held its color, and he wasn't about to let what he and his colleagues had worked so hard to build fade away, either. Perhaps one of the biggest corporate decisions made under Earl Wyman was to expand manufacturing capability outside the state of Wisconsin. In 1953, he decided to go ahead with plans to build a brand new manufacturing facility in Celina, Tennessee. Wyman, with his long-standing relationship with the union label, wanted the union in Celina, too. It was here they would make pants and shirts and increase their capacity to manufacture multipurpose clothes for work and play.

Before 1956 came to a close, the success of Earl Wyman's calculated risk in Celina was self-evident. The original 30,000-square-foot building was busting at the seams, and the decision was made to add another 15,000 square feet, the first of six additions to be made over the years. At the same time, processes were modernized to give the company the industry's leadership role as the proud owner of one of the most efficient plants in the needle trade.

New OshKosh B'Gosh styles demonstrated that the company was working to maintain its status as the outfitter of the American worker by providing stylish, functional, comfortable workwear.

This 1951 ad, left, shows the variety of coats, bibs, work shirts and other apparel produced by OshKosh. The famous engineer's cap, below, is sold across the country and is recognized everywhere.

The fashion pendulum, however, swings both ways. By the close of this illustrious decade, filled with new music and ambitious new attitudes, the famous BRONKS, along with other better-known brands such as Levi's® or Lee®, would suddenly be shunned.

Whether it was Elvis Presley, the growing underground culture of the beatniks or the image of tough guys played on screen by Marlon Brando or James Dean, mothers, fathers and local school boards figured blue jeans were too much a symbol of rebellion and mustn't be worn in school. Yes, it's true, there was a time blue jeans were outlawed, rendered inappropriate for school attire. Sales of blue jeans slowed, but management at OshKosh adapted and turned their energies to developing their men's wear product lines away from the ever-popular blue denim.

Sales growth wasn't anything to write home about during the last five years of the 1950s. Still, posting net sales of $5.8 million in 1956 and $6.2 million at the close of 1960 suggests that despite the changes on the retail side of the counter, the demand for high-quality, rugged and fashionable work and casual wear remained.

Fashion wasn't the only force bringing change to the company. Early in the 1960s, OshKosh B'Gosh faced a major production challenge. To insure profitability, it was important to be frugal in purchasing materials and to waste as little fabric as possible. An efficient design and cutting process was essential to curb waste. While typical machinery upgrades were introduced and the normal course of modernization proceeded, the design and basic fabrics remained unchanged.

Two significant events confronted the company in 1963. The first came when the company's sole pattern and design maker came down with a debilitating illness that forced him to leave, and the second arrived in the form of a strike by textile workers at the company's largest denim supplier. To avoid interrupting production, other suppliers were sought out. Both situations challenged the new management team of Fritz Hyde and Tom Wyman, as well as the hard-working men and women who had been used to doing things consistently for years and were forced to re-think and retool. Change isn't always easy.

Fritz Hyde became the president of OshKosh B'Gosh in 1963, smack dab in the middle of what felt like a crisis. Tom Wyman sought out other suppliers while Fritz Hyde went looking for a new pattern and design maker.

Tom Wyman, shown at left on the manufacturing floor, recognized the need to change to keep pace with customers' needs. Under his leadership, OshKosh introduced many new product lines such as the BRONKS jeans pictured in the ad below.

IF YOU ADMIRE SHARP ATTIRE

OshKosh
CASUALS

As Americans enjoyed their postwar affluence, they developed new patterns of work and play. For OshKosh B'Gosh to make the transition from workwear to casual wear that would satisfy postwar consumers required new ideas and new people. The ad above, in its portrayal of leisure and clean-cut fashion, hints at the culltural change in the country and the company.

CHAPTER SIX

FROM TAILORED SUITS TO BIB OVERALLS

THOUGH there are many stories of the American Dream fulfilled at OshKosh B'Gosh, it's clear that the hardworking nature of those who immigrated to the United States has had its influence on the success of this company. Of all these stories, there is one in particular that carries with it all of the common threads of such a dream.

Anthony S. Giordano was born in Italy just as Benito Mussolini marched in goose-step with Adolph Hitler to form their ideological alliance of destruction. The war came to its end when he was eight years old. It seems he grew up with a needle, thread and scissors in his hand and a goal to become one of the finest tailors in all the land.

In the winter of 1958, at the age of 21, Tony set sail for New York City. This American dream was to take him to Madison Avenue, Manhattan, in the heart of the most important city in the world. Sidetracked by an invitation to apprentice in Milwaukee, Tony accepted even though it would take him away from New York, believing it would only be temporary and just a stepping stone along the way. After all, the shop in Milwaukee made suits for some of the industrial leaders of the day— men with names like Bradley, Stratton and Kasten who wore only the finest suits made to their personal satisfaction.

Milwaukee did prove to be a short stop for the youthful Tony Giordano. He returned to New York in 1959 to attend the Cybick School of Design where he earned his degree in clothing and textile design in 1961. Then he accepted a position as assistant designer for a renowned sports and casual wear manufacturer in New Jersey. Though he was doing what he set out to do, it meant leaving his girlfriend behind in Milwaukee.

After about a year and a half, the gravitational pull back to Milwaukee grew too strong to resist. Tony responded to a classified ad in a trade journal placed by a small company in Oshkosh, Wisconsin, that was looking for someone with his type of background. All he knew at the time was that anywhere in Wisconsin couldn't be too far from Milwaukee.

Frtiz Hyde and Anthony Giordano met in a small New Jersey tavern not far from where Tony worked in the spring or early summer of 1963. Fritz took a liking to Tony and hired him on the spot. It would be a month or so before Giordano would report to OshKosh B'Gosh. Anticipating what things would need to be done upon arrival at his new job, he prepared himself through additional schooling that would ultimately pay

himself and the company ample dividends.

At the outset, Giordano figured he would help the company for two or three years and then move on. However, he had met the love of his life in Milwaukee, who would soon become his bride. And the excitement of working for a growing company moving from workwear to casual wear to a dominant maker of fashionable children's wear would hold his attention, devotion and commitment for more than 30 years without interruption. Tony had arrived on Otter Avenue to stay.

By the time Tony arrived, Tom Wyman had a new denim supplier to replace the one that had gone on strike. Adjusting manufacturing methods to the various widths of the new bolts of denim now in use at the company posed a challenge to a long-established mind-set and methodology within OshKosh. The adjustment period could cost hundreds of thousands of dollars in wasted time and fabric yardage, not to mention productivity.

Giordano quickly established himself as the new design manager. Tom Wyman noted, "Tony was solely responsible" for enabling the company to pay for the new technology it acquired within a six-month period. This new and leading-edge technology, known as Tex-O-Graph, was created to mini-

mize waste and achieve better utilization of fabric. OshKosh B'Gosh was perhaps the first manufacturer in the country to incorporate its use.

When asked about this period of time, Giordano takes little credit, believing he did nothing more than what he had been hired to do. In speaking of those early days, Tony said, "Though they [Earl Wyman, Tom Wyman and Fritz Hyde] were watching me, I think I gained their trust." His comment is something of an understatement. In 1973, the company appointed him manager of corporate quality assurance. In January 1980, Tony was given the title and responsibility of vice president of manufacturing. Today, as a senior executive officer of the company, Tony S. Giordano, the boy from Italy, has played an intricate role in setting the stage for the company's strategic plans for manufacturing their goods globally. Tony is just one of

What is there about Paris that's so American?

Bull Denim® from Graniteville

OshKosh CASUALS
OSHKOSH B'GOSH INC. OSHKOSH, WISCONSIN

RELAX IN RUGGED
DRESS-UP WESTERNS

OshKosh
dudes

- TRIM SLIM FIT
- BRASS NO-SCRATCH RIVETS
- ZIPPER FLY
- SANFORIZED
- RUGGED STITCHED
- EXTRA HEAVY COTTON THUNDERCORD
- RUGGED WEAR WITH EASY CARE

$3.50

many who found OshKosh B'Gosh a rewarding place to pursue and live the American Dream.

Over the years, many like Giordano have come to Osh-Kosh B'Gosh to spend virtually their entire working careers. To single Tony out among the many is to describe only a small part of what has become an international story. Those who know the company realize that there have been many loyal, hard-working members of this team over the years who have contributed to its past and have laid the groundwork for what is envisioned as an exciting future.

As new fabrics were catching on in the United States, Europeans were finding a fascination for American casual wear and developing a penchant for wearing a pair of all-American "dudes" from OshKosh B'Gosh.

Consider the well-dressed limb

Adorned in a tasteful assortment of The Guys, preferred profile pants, it poses the vexing hangup: What to wear today? . . . slacks or jeans? . . . striped, plaid or plain? Solution: With your own assortment of The Guys you're covered for any occasion, casual or dress. And that beats sitting around in your skivvies. So vex a little. At The Guys' prices you can afford it.

If you are 40 or under— around the waist— The Guys are your slacks

Being able to wear The Guys isn't a matter of luck. If you've been wise enough to keep your chest bigger than your stomach — The Guys are for you. You look good, they look good on you. The Guys are lastingly Best/Prest. Get to wear The Guys!

The Guys preferred profile pants

CHAPTER SEVEN

NEW KIDS AND FANCY COLORS

IN THE EARLY 1960s, societal changes made their mark on the company. It had become obvious that agricultural and railroad workers' needs were no longer the sole driving force behind the company's product lines.

There were people in the company who were watching the movement from rural to urban areas, and some of them thought the name OshKosh B'Gosh should be taken off all of the non-workwear products. They believed to most consumers it represented the farm, the country — Hicksville — and that young people in particular just weren't fascinated by barnyards. So, in an effort to avoid an identity crisis and to capitalize on consumer demand for more comfortable casual wear, The Guys brand name was introduced. The Guys identified a new line of boy's and men's washed pants.

Permanent press and polyester fabrics arrived, as did the now infamous men's leisure suits. The company responded conservatively to the leisure suit concept and to new technology and fabric applications. It's well that they were cautious, for looking back at pictures taken of men in permanent press and polyester pants reminds us of a time thankfully past.

By the mid-1960s, shifting demographics forced the color of OshKosh B'Gosh to change forever. The social revolution that stormed the country accompanied a demographic change over which sociologists continue to marvel. The younger generation was large, affluent, inquisitive and willing to experiment. While the company was busy figuring out how to update its image, young adults everywhere in the United States were trying to figure out who they were and why they were.

A lyricist asked, "Are you going to San Francisco? Be sure to wear some flowers in your hair." Along with flowers in their hair, they wore OshKosh B'Gosh denim bib overalls. On the East Coast, when thousands gathered on a rural hillside near Woodstock, New York, the media pictured many a smiling face above a body clothed in a pair of bibs. The revolution put on a new uniform: both young men and women wore their bib overalls in solidarity with the working class, or maybe just because they were easy to get in and out of.

Meanwhile, back in Oshkosh, no one knew what all of this would lead to, but to be sure, Earl Wyman wasn't going to allow his two younger protégés to assume that the recent craze was a long-term trend. Rather, the company's leaders were often reminded to go at it conservatively. If the trend were to continue, the company would respond, but if it turned out to be a short-lived fad, they would not find themselves caught with unsold and costly inventory. Work clothing and durable outerwear, predominantly of heavy denim and twill fabrics, were still the mainstay, and the company's roots held firm through the shifting fashion currents in casual wear.

Whether their overalls came from second-hand stores or grandpa's attic, the youth of America, during the 1960s and 70s, found a special delight in the uniform American farmers had worn for generations.

And then came kids, small kids. Even in the very early days, the company had offered children the opportunity to dress just like their dads, but selling kids bib overalls produced kid-size commission checks. Another company, Miles Kimball Co., was largely responsible for initiating the marketing effort that would ultimately make kids an important part of the next decade or so for OshKosh B'Gosh.

It was in the early 1960s when the marketing folks at Miles Kimball decided to use a picture of a cute child wearing OshKosh B'Gosh-made hickory-striped overalls in their catalog. The consumer took notice. Recognizing the opportunity, Fritz Hyde developed a marketing brochure to capitalize on the wide publicity the Miles Kimball catalog created. The brochure, featuring two bibs, two painter pants, two chore coats and two caps in sizes one through ten, was sent directly to specialty children's clothing stores across the country. It wasn't long before toddlers on Fifth Avenue in New York

City were seen in OshKosh B'Gosh bib overalls. It's hard to recollect who called first: whether it was a Bloomingdale's buyer or a Saks Fifth Avenue buyer, Fritz Hyde and Tom Wyman knew something was up. Before you could say, "Frank Grove, Howie Jenkins, Jim Clark, Bill Pollock and Earl Wyman," the world of children's fashion would demand the rainbow, and OshKosh B'Gosh would deliver it.

To talk about the years to follow without mention of Jack Beckman is like serving hot apple cider without the cinnamon stick. In 1975, word was that OshKosh B'Gosh was looking for the right person to direct the company's sales effort. With almost 30 years of experience in the apparel business, Beckman knew OshKosh B'Gosh well.

Jack Beckman had been associated with companies primarily in the southern United States, and would be the first to tell you that whenever he attempted to push north of Omaha, Nebraska, he found

competition with OshKosh B'Gosh real tough. Holding the company in high regard, Jack put himself in the running for the sales management position, and Fritz Hyde sensed Beckman was the right person for the job. At the time, children's wear made up less than eight percent of total revenues. Although there had been some effort to expand sales beyond the upper Midwest, what the company really needed was someone to take it south of Iowa, east of Chicago and over the Rocky Mountains in a meaningful way.

Jack Beckman found 12 salesmen and five manufacturer's reps working for OshKosh when he arrived. Though he realized there was much work to do, his vast experience and large number of contacts in the apparel industry served the company well. The decision to open a regional sales office in Chicago came first. Because Jack had spent many years with office space in New York, he saw that location as the next priority. Reluctant at first, management finally approved, and Beckman plugged in phones and set up typewriters and a support staff a few blocks from the Empire State Building

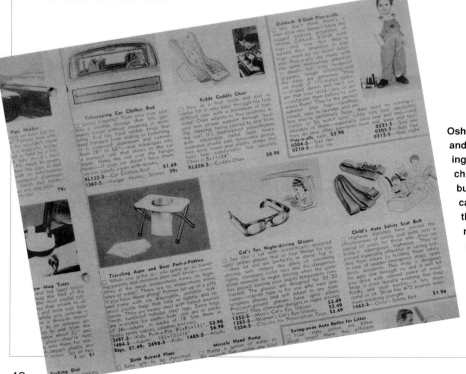

OshKosh had been making overalls for children and had been using children in their advertising since 1910. Miles Kimball first featured children's bib overalls in their 1962 catalog, but it was nearly a decade later that their catalog started a trend that has continued to the present. Children have become the major focus of OshKosh B'Gosh, and the honesty and freshness of children's faces has replaced the face of the American worker as the image of the OshKosh customer.

in the heart of New York's commercial center. With a chuckle, he recalls vividly Hyde's comment at the time the new regional office opened: "The only thing I'm worried about, Jack, is that it will be too easy for people to find us out there. We'll lose that wonderful OshKosh mystique."

Beckman knew what his boss meant, but he also knew that if this company were to make the most of the fashion trend, that now looked to be far more than a passing fad, it was critical for OshKosh B'Gosh to be readily accessible to the New York crowd. In his experience, no one had ever produced a line of clothing that had as much integrity or quality. In speaking with buyers, he found they were absolutely fascinated with what he refers to as the "sincerity of the line — they simply were not accustomed to finding that high level of quality."

Despite the fact that there were actually few colors and styles to choose from, it became chic for folks to send their children off to school wearing bib overalls in blue denim, hickory stripes or best of all,

the basic primary colors. The manufacturing and selling process was easier then, since there were probably as few as seven or eight lot numbers to choose from. That number would grow into the hundreds, even thousands, as time passed.

The company enjoyed sales of just under $17 million when Jack Beckman arrived, and by the time he retired in 1991, sales exceeded $365 million. On the way to such lofty heights, Beckman once said to Fritz Hyde, "You know, Fritz, I'm not sure how high is up, but we're probably going to find out."

Midway into his career at OshKosh B'Gosh, a longtime friend and professional acquaintance who did the buying for Macy's in New York City wanted to send a package to Jack in Oshkosh. Noting that he had the post office box of the company but not the street address, Jack gave it to him, "112 Otter Avenue."

The buyer responded, "Otter Avenue? Gee, I don't think we even have an Otter Avenue in New York." Reminded that there were a lot of things New York didn't have, the buyer, a wry grin on his face, then said, "Well, Jack,

It was clear that children were wearing OshKosh bib overalls, but the real consumers who emerged in the eighties were the parents and grandparents of those children. Not only did children look adorable in the bibs, but the clothes held up to the beating kids can give their wardrobe. Once OshKosh realized how much appreciation their children's line was earning, marketing efforts increasingly featured overall-clad youngsters.

looks to me like the otters are going to eat up the alligators" — referring to the famed logo of IZOD®, one of the major producers of children's wear made so popular during that time.

Demand outstripped supply as success multiplied. During that time period, however, none of the company's managers, including Beckman, ever grew complacent. One thing he had learned over his years in the business was that a manufacturer of clothing lines "stood for election three times a year: in the spring, in the fall and during the holiday period. If you happened to 'lose an election,' no amount of loyalty could keep you in the running." The fashion business is a fickle place to make a living and the leaders of this company respected that. The future growth of OshKosh B'Gosh was not guaranteed. It was Jack Beckman's job to see to it that wherever the product could be sold, it was.

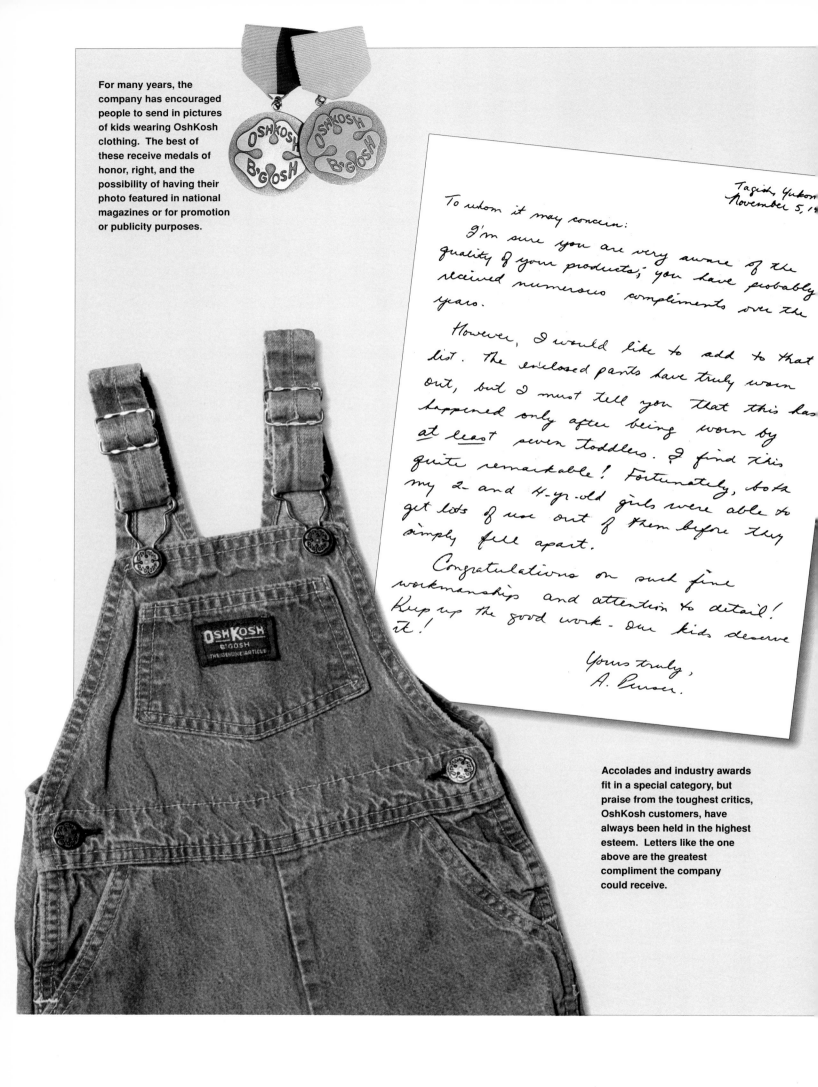

For many years, the company has encouraged people to send in pictures of kids wearing OshKosh clothing. The best of these receive medals of honor, right, and the possibility of having their photo featured in national magazines or for promotion or publicity purposes.

Tagish, Yukon
November 5, 19

To whom it may concern:

I'm sure you are very aware of the quality of your products; you have probably received numerous compliments over the years.

However, I would like to add to that list. The enclosed pants have truly worn out, but I must tell you that this has happened only after being worn by _at least_ seven toddlers. I find this quite remarkable! Fortunately, both my 2- and 4-yr.-old girls were able to get lots of use out of them before they simply fell apart.

Congratulations on such fine workmanship and attention to detail! Keep up the good work. Our kids deserve it!

Yours truly,
A. Purser.

Accolades and industry awards fit in a special category, but praise from the toughest critics, OshKosh customers, have always been held in the highest esteem. Letters like the one above are the greatest compliment the company could receive.

CHAPTER EIGHT

THOSE HEADY YEARS

Bill Wyman, son of Tom Wyman and grandson of Earl Wyman, began as a salesman for OshKosh and is now part of the management team.

YOU REMEMBER Miriam Knaggs who first came to work for the company in 1929. Miriam has watched the generations come and go, and she carries in her mind a treasure chest of memories. She remembers young Bill Wyman, grandson of Earl, coming around as a youngster. While in high school, young Wyman worked on the shipping and receiving dock. Miriam teased the growing lad as he struggled with large cardboard boxes he was instructed to break down and bale in the receiving area.

Bill has a lot of memories of his own. Before he was old enough and big enough to work, young Wyman ventured with his father, Tom, to the plant on Saturdays. With the place quiet in weekend slumber, Bill would jump in the canvas bins that sat atop conveyor lines and ride with glee, happy that nobody worked on the only day he was able to visit.

Twenty years later, young Bill would be identified in the company's annual report as W.F. Wyman, Vice President— Domestic Licensing. He didn't arrive at that position overnight. After his college years, Bill was happy to receive the opportunity to take on a sales territory first in Indianapolis and later in Sacramento, California. Though a long distance from home, everything he learned over the years stayed with him, and he found that the strength of the OshKosh B'Gosh name opened many a door. Now a member of the company's energetic management team, Bill Wyman's experience strengthens his resolve to preserve the character and strength of a globally recognized brand name.

After 44 years of employment, Miriam Knaggs walked the floor of OshKosh B'Gosh in 1973 for the last time. Lois Van Dien's career with the company began about that time. She, like Miriam, started in a temporary job that she expected to be just that — short. Lois can tell you how things have changed, having moved from the Tex-O-Graph department to the high-tech world of computerized marking and pattern design. Lois knows what it means when one speaks of the quality that goes into every OshKosh B'Gosh garment. In her twenty-second year with OshKosh B'Gosh, she's put in only half the time Miriam did, but has learned to live and dream with all those others who put many years of dedicated service into the company they've come to love. Lois arrived when great things were about to happen and she's still here to talk about it today. She talks with a sense of anticipation, as if she clearly sees the direction the company is headed and could not be more excited. Others share her enthusiasm.

Two years after Lois arrived, Doug Hyde, who was working for a large defense contractor, was invited to join the firm. A sales territory including Madison, Wisconsin, opened up, and the firm's president, Doug's father, Fritz, offered him the opportunity to take it over. Though Doug had grown up among the family members who ran the company, he wasn't sure his connection with it would go beyond the high school and college jobs he held there. If ever there was a time to find out, this was it. Doug accepted.

By the time Doug arrived, children were being dressed in bib overalls that were just like the ones farmers and railroad men had worn for 80 years — tough, durable, indestructible. Doug Hyde quickly found his niche as a salesman, but when he looked closely at the product he was selling, he wasn't convinced that kids needed bib overalls made the same way they'd been made for years.

There was no question that mothers would still insist on the same durability and quality, but as far as Doug was concerned, a different approach to fabrics and styling might make The Genuine Article® even better. After all, it wasn't just little boys who were wearing bibs, and if little girls could choose from a variety of pretty patterns, who says they wouldn't love them?

Before Doug became the director of merchandising for the firm, Jack Beckman recognized that Doug had a real talent for merchandising and a terrific natural ability to understand color and classic detail. According to Beckman, "Doug Hyde knew well how to produce a substantial, solid, honest type of children's product, and he did it very well."

The more Doug Hyde learned from his customers and ultimate consumers, the more

ideas he brought to the company's leaders. What about snaps up the legs of children's bibs — then diaper changers wouldn't have to get the kids all the way out of their bibs to do the job? What about a softer fabric, more supple and comfortable? In addition to becoming one of the company's premier salesmen, it was evident to his supervisors and industry peers that Doug had a knack for merchandising. The kid who wasn't sure about his role at OshKosh had climbed aboard as if red bandana and denim bibs were his uniform. He was ready to stoke the engine and ride the rails beyond his wildest dreams.

During his years as a salesman in Madison, Doug Hyde and his brother-in-law-to-be, Mike Wachtel, roomed together for a time. Doug's younger sister, Margaret (everybody calls her "Peg"), had fallen in love with Mike, her high school sweetheart, who was attending the University of Wisconsin and planned to become a pharmacist. He had the skills and a sense of curiosity that drove him to investigate technical complexities. Pharmacy was something he knew he could enjoy. He envisioned himself behind the counter of a corner drug store, serving his local community's needs.

There is now a generation of mothers who were dressed in bibs themselves. In a fast-paced modern society, the wholesome image of sun-tanned, barefoot children romping around in OshKosh B'Gosh overalls is a sight from the past that strikes a nostalgic and appealing chord for many people. These two winners of the 1989-90 photo contest, Jonathan and Kristina, grace the front of postcards conveying such an image of a happy, healthy childhood.

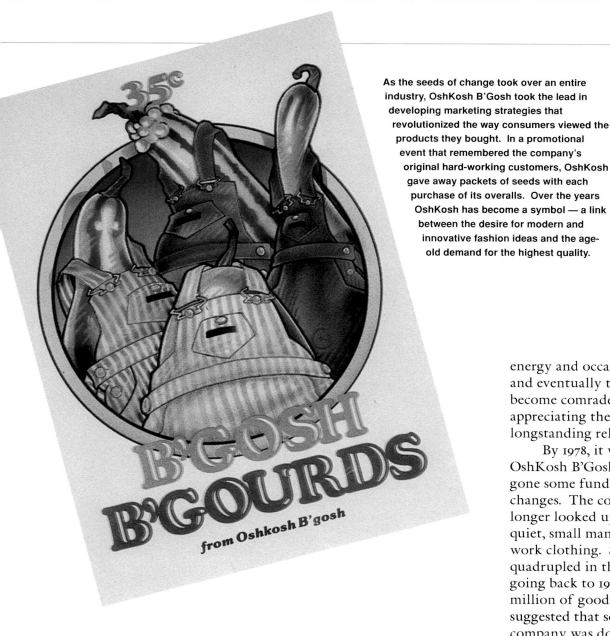

35¢

B'GOSH B'GOURDS

from Oshkosh B'gosh

As the seeds of change took over an entire industry, OshKosh B'Gosh took the lead in developing marketing strategies that revolutionized the way consumers viewed the products they bought. In a promotional event that remembered the company's original hard-working customers, OshKosh gave away packets of seeds with each purchase of its overalls. Over the years OshKosh has become a symbol — a link between the desire for modern and innovative fashion ideas and the age-old demand for the highest quality.

energy and occasional rivalry, and eventually they would become comrades-at-arms, fully appreciating the value of their longstanding relationship.

By 1978, it was clear that OshKosh B'Gosh had undergone some fundamental changes. The company was no longer looked upon as just a quiet, small manufacturer of work clothing. Sales had quadrupled in the 15-year period going back to 1963. The $26 million of goods sold in 1978 suggested that something the company was doing was right.

Fritz Hyde and Tom Wyman were not about to let this success go to their heads. Rather than building up huge inventories, they attempted to anticipate consumer demands and manufacture product accordingly. Because it was no longer a case of one or two styles, but rather what seemed like a myriad of new colors and as many design specifications, the last thing management wanted was warehouses stacked to the ceiling with kids' bib overalls and no place to ship them. Some wondered if this trend was just another blip on the screen of the ever-fickle American consumer.

Mike and Peg eventually attended the university together, spending time with brother Doug. In spite of the family connection, the couple never really thought seriously about ever being a part of the OshKosh B'Gosh story. They are very much a part of this story today. When Fritz Hyde suffered a heart attack in 1979, Mike had already accepted a sales position with the company, working a northern Wisconsin territory. "If only pine trees wore overalls," Mike laments. "But you know, I did have the most sales per capita of any of the sales reps." Now there's a positive thinker for

you! When Fritz became ill, he asked Mike to return to Oshkosh to become his personal assistant. Since his father-in-law was ordered to stay flat on his back in bed for a prolonged period of time, Mike found himself with serious responsibilities. He handled them well.

It's always hard to step into a serious role, but being the chief executive's son-in-law presents certain challenges common to siblings within any family business. Both Mike and Doug Hyde had much to learn about dealing with those who questioned their abilities. They both grew through some of the painful days of youthful

Also in 1978, Earl Wyman passed away. He never officially retired from the company, and although he had turned full operating responsibility over to others, his interest in it was keen. Those who worked with him still praise his ability to foresee and plan for growth. He instilled in his subordinates the need to fully assess and minimize risk and take only those risks that promised sufficient profit.

Earl Wyman's legacy remains. By 1981, sales had increased 100 percent from 1978. They doubled again by mid-1983, and again by 1986, to more than $198 million. Bill Jacobson, Ken Masters, Bobby Morrison and legions of others helped manage this extraordinary growth.

In order to meet the demands, the company had built six plants since the first out-of-state operation in Celina, Tennessee, went into production in 1953. The expansion would not end there. Eleven more plants were opened during the eighties. Demand actually exceeded supply. These were very exciting times, and everyone at the company knew it. The spending habits of a citizenry gone upscale in the eighties were much to the company's advantage.

Young, upwardly mobile professionals were having children at a time when people of their class were bent on dressing and driving in only the best. As they acquired BMW's, their kids wore bib overalls. There was status in both, for just as BMW's were pricey, so too were the hottest kids' fashion item of the century. They were manufactured in plants in small, rural communities in Tennessee, Kentucky and, of course, Oshkosh, far away from the glitz and glamour of Rodeo Drive in Beverly Hills or Fifth Avenue in New York.

To the money moguls, mavens and Wall Street types whose kids sported the bib overalls, the hand-stitched blue denim patch, embroidered with bright yellow thread read not "OshKosh B'Gosh — The Genuine Article Since 1895®," but rather, "There must be money in them thar' overalls!" Wall Street came a' knocking. The company's product was everywhere, and investment bankers finally convinced management that the time was right to restructure their capital and offer stock, albeit in a form that would maintain the voting strength the family desired.

William Blair & Company was retained to handle the deal, which took place in May of 1985, and the stock began trading, opening on the NASDAQ (National Association of Securities Dealers Automated Quote) system or over-the-counter market. In investment parlance, the stock traded under the symbol GOSHA and became one of the "darling" deals of the year.

Though the numbers were exciting and the profits big, the last person convinced of fashion's constancy was Fritz Hyde. In his 1986 annual report, Hyde opened his letter to shareholders with the statement, "Thank heaven for little kids whose parents, grandparents and friends made our year." He went on to note that net income had grown by almost 47 percent over the previous year and earnings per common share had grown by better than 50 percent.

OshKosh B'Gosh has endeavored to fit just about anybody and anything into a pair of their world-famous bib-overalls. "Tough as a mule's hide" and sequined to fit the occasion, this pair is gracefully modeled by a cast member of the Cabrini Circus.

Though initiated in 1981 as a means of selling imperfect garments and overruns and not considered part of the grander scheme of the company's worldwide growth, the retail outlet stores had also produced a 50 percent increase in sales over the previous year. Numbers like these could not go unnoticed by Wall Street.

Fritz Hyde, guarded and tempered in his optimism, told shareholders, "Your company is monitoring very closely major changes taking place in the retail marketplace, changes which seem to be accelerating. Mergers, acquisitions, and leveraged buyouts have changed retailers' sourcing strategies and presented us with challenges that we are positioning our marketing forces to meet. In the confused and competitive retail scene — with no consensus on promoting branded or private label apparel, with retailers doing manufacturing and manufacturers doing retailing — there are no certain paths to success. We are ready to meet the new challenges this marketplace presents and will benefit from new opportunities."

Five years later, in 1991, sales peaked at $365 million. Charles "Fritz" Hyde vacated the president's office, making room for his successor, Douglas W. Hyde. Doug's accession to the presidency was greeted with mixed reactions. Some considered him a "superstar," others looked at him with suspicion. They wondered if he was just the boss's son, who happened to have a hot streak selling in a favorable environment, or if he was a talented manager who was the right choice to lead OshKosh in the nineties and beyond.

Pick up a magazine that carries an OshKosh B'Gosh ad and it is tough to pass the page without stopping to smile at the cute kids. The ads feature real kids involved in real activities — at the beach, in a leaf pile, or wherever — simply enjoying being kids.

A lot can change in a century. At OshKosh, the number of employees has increased many times over, the process of making clothes has been radically transformed, and products come in new sizes, styles, fabrics and colors. OshKosh has accommodated such changes while keeping its traditional values intact. It continues to produce the highest quality of clothing and to offer its employees opportunities that help them realize their dreams.

CHAPTER NINE

BEYOND THE CENTENNIAL

E VERY MANAGER has a distinct style. When he ran the company, William Pollock kept his eye on productivity and was known to ask a pausing seamstress if there was a reason why she wasn't busy. Earl Wyman knew everyone who worked for him. As he strolled the factory floor on one of his many visits throughout a typical day, he'd greet his workmates by name.

Fritz Hyde, a tall, distinguished-looking executive, managed forthrightly, but quietly. Douglas Hyde, on the other hand, though 40 years old when he became president, was looked upon as a young executive yet to be tested. Although he had already earned the respect of industry insiders, the skeptics on Wall Street had to be convinced.

One thing Doug Hyde learned over the years was that just being a part of the family would never be enough to meet the demands of shareholders. While heritage might once have been sufficient to command the corner office, Doug and other family members care most that the right people get the best jobs, regardless of family connections. "Being in the family might get you an interview and a chance at bat, but the rest depends on what you've accom-

Most manufacturing operations have been changed dramatically by technological developments in the late twentieth century, and the clothing business is no exception. Above, new processes allow workers to cut out larger quantities of pattern pieces at one time, vastly speeding the preparation process, though all garments are still sewn by hand.

plished, not who you are," says one family member. A consummate sales professional, Doug Hyde also knew when he stepped into the presidency that it would take a great deal more than kinetic energy to take OshKosh beyond the recent years that had been so good to the company and everyone involved with it: employees and shareholders alike.

The simple truth was that during the 1980s, making money was pretty easy — OshKosh B'Gosh seemed to be on everyone's shopping list. Making money in the nineties would

require different disciplines, different strategies and a rejuvenated and invigorated management team to pull it all off. Doug Hyde and Mike Wachtel put a lean new team together. It included Bill Wyman and a close-knit group of other senior managers who shared the new vision of the company. Doug would eventually serve in his current position, president and chief executive officer, while Mike would become executive vice president and chief operating officer. Together, they would form the nucleus of the next

In the clothing industry, those "in the know" know Doug Hyde. He is respected as a leader ready to introduce OshKosh B'Gosh clothing to yet another generation of customers.

generation. Filled with youthful energy, they were determined to take what had become a $365 million company to the next level, despite the reality that the yuppie parents of the eighties were gone. Buying habits among Americans had changed dramatically, and no longer would retailers be willing to wait in line for OshKosh B'Gosh products when competitors' less expensive items would do.

Transitions are difficult, no matter who's in charge. Company sales slipped from $365 million in 1991 to $346 million in 1992 and $340 million in 1993. Shareholders at the 1993 annual meeting, in the spring of 1994, were told about plant closings, employee layoffs, balance sheet

restructuring items and acquisition deals that had fallen through. Shareholder Ted Sutherland stood up following management's presentation and wondered aloud if the company had really learned anything from the past year or two. It was a legitimate question; others were wondering the same thing.

Doug Hyde not only addressed the question about what had been learned, but also shared a glimpse of the future. In essence, his response indicated that the new team of managers had thought deeply about the issues facing the company, and yes, they had benefited greatly from the lessons of the past. In 1994, retail sales of OshKosh B'Gosh products in

Who ever said that "sturdy" clothes couldn't look nice? It's fun to have the best of both worlds, and OshKosh B'Gosh is all it takes.

When Ronald Reagan came to Oshkosh in 1985, he recognized the world's only Genuine Article as an example of the value and quality that years of dedicated attention to detail are able to produce. The president promised to wear his new bibs upon returning to his ranch in Santa Barbara, California, and word has it, he did — many times.

international markets amounted to approximately $75 million according to Hyde, and as far as he was concerned, that number should more than quadruple by the year 2000. Additionally, what most observers didn't realize was that the number of OshKosh B'Gosh retail outlet stores had grown from the two company stores that Fritz Hyde referred to in his 1986 report to shareholders, to 61 stores at the close of 1994. If all goes as planned, there will be another 20 or so operating when the company celebrates its centennial. These outlets produced over 18 percent of revenues in 1994. Judging from current performances, Doug Hyde firmly believes the opportunities both abroad and here in the United States are enormous.

Doug Hyde works on the fourth floor of corporate headquarters in a tastefully decorated office where an E. Ingraham "Regulator" clock tick-

When people from around the globe think about the typical life in rural America — the farms, the open spaces, the tire swinging from an old oak tree — more often than not they also envision kids dressed in The Genuine Article.

As executive vice president and chief operating officer, Mike Wachtel shares with Doug Hyde the challenge of steering OshKosh into the next century. The market has changed since the frenzied days of the 1980s, but they have identified promising opportunities for the company's future growth.

tocks, measuring the hours he spends steering OshKosh B'Gosh into the next hundred years. He and his counterpart, Mike Wachtel, whose office is at the opposite end of the hallway, have no misconceptions about who they are and where they must take this company. Doug Hyde does have a vision and describes himself as "being more excited about the business opportunities today than I was back in the go-go years." This enthusiasm comes from his appetite for the task ahead: to work with the members of his team to lead and shape OshKosh B'Gosh.

In the past, many a new manager was snatched from an unrelated department as a new need arose in the burgeoning business. Someone from distribution, for instance, might be tapped to fill an important catalog slot, despite the fact that the person was needed in distribution and had no experience in direct sales. While this practice worked some of the time, other times it failed to

provide the company with the sophisticated expertise these new operations required. As Doug Hyde would point out, "Strategies don't mean anything unless you have the right people to implement them." The hiring process was formalized in the mid-eighties, and since then, managers have been proven professionals, respected in their fields and able to bring a depth of industry expertise to the opportunities that face OshKosh.

This team constantly examines all growth opportunities that could maximize the company's broad franchise. Some managers look at the international sales and licensing arrangements similar to the ones Jack Beckman initiated; others explore licensing, direct markets, new distribution arrangements, showcase retail stores such as the one on New York City's Fifth Avenue, new wholesaling opportunities and global sourcing. It has been a period during which both the product side and the people side

People who play hard have the same need for tough, durable clothes as those who work hard. OshKosh continues to outfit people for both work and play in the same solid product for which the company has always been known.

of the business have changed to meet changing conditions.

The impact of these new men and women has been dramatic. New strategies have been implemented along with new marketing approaches. One of these new focuses has involved a return to the original roots of the company: the production of traditional men's workwear. The classic five-pocket jean leads this division of clothing along with an increased selection of men's outerwear, flannel shirts and new casual wear that meets the Saturday night and other non-workday needs of customers. This effort, which has included a separate sales force and advertising campaign, has proved to be well worth it; sales in men's wear grew 16 percent from 1993 to 1994.

The fashion world embraced the basic concept of solid, rugged children's wear exemplified by the classic bib overalls — then asked for more. OshKosh's creative design and merchandising strategies delivered the rainbow.

Pictures say it better than words. Cute kids dressed in colorful outfits are a part of today's OshKosh story — woven in all the traditions and images from the past.

There is no doubt that OshKosh's bread and butter is children's clothing. OshKosh wholesale children's wear is the largest segment of the business; the second is OshKosh B'Gosh retail. Another new marketing approach that has quickly grown into the third largest segment of the company's business is the new brand, Genuine Kids™.

Though the brand is new, the idea isn't. In 1990, OshKosh acquired Essex Outfitters and began manufacturing children's clothing under the Boston Trader brand name. This line was distributed by Essex, primarily in outlet stores called Trader Kids. Sales grew dramatically in the early 1990s.

When the licensing agreement that allowed Essex to use the Boston Trader name ended in 1994, OshKosh was determined to keep the successful

venture operating. The business was renamed Genuine Kids and the retail outlet stores were renamed Genuine Kids, as well.

The line reaches more affluent consumers than OshKosh's other children's wear brands. While Genuine Kids includes clothing for newborn to 16, more than half of sales come from the 7 to 16 size category. Seventy-seven stores were in operation at the end of 1994, including one mall-based specialty store.

In addition to increased domestic success, OshKosh has been forging ahead with international licensing agreements and sales abroad. Though breaking into Europe has brought with it some unexpected challenges, the company is on track in its effort to cultivate its reputation for high quality, reliability and design excellence — characteristics consumers throughout the world have come to expect from the OshKosh B'Gosh brand.

Sales and licensing revenues now come from more than 70 countries, and the list is growing. OshKosh has become a diversified global children's wear company with broad penetration and astounding brand recognition. New marketing strategies, be they vertical, horizontal or in totally new categories, will sustain growth throughout the decade and beyond.

OshKosh B'Gosh children's wear is the leading brand in Canada, Australia, Singapore, Korea, Chile and Argentina. In order to establish the name and set the standard for the proper brand image, the company opened retail outlets in London and Paris. OshKosh is currently considering other European

The new brand, Genuine Kids, has grown into the third largest segment of OshKosh's business by appealing to upscale consumers.

The OshKosh B'Gosh photo contest went international in the nineties. This bronze metal-winning photograph from the 1992-93 photo contest shows OshKosh's international line of children's wear, which is available in over 70 countries.

outlets, and in 1993, the company established a subsidiary in Hong Kong to help manage business on the other side of the globe. The emerging markets offer considerable opportunity, and consumers in places like India and Pakistan, among many others, are changing rapidly in their desire to purchase high-quality products. Without question, OshKosh B'Gosh intends to be there.

From a company with sales of under $400 million in 1994 — as Doug Hyde and his management team know —The Genuine Article, born and bred at OshKosh over the last hundred years, will be a company with sales looking at the billion dollar mark before he and his cohorts hang up their bib overalls for good.

The Common Threads of an American Dream

There's something to be said about reviewing history and all the stories that go along with it. To travel the roads a company and its people have traversed not only serves the purpose of rekindling fond memories, but provides the backdrop for those who peer into the future. Frank Grove probably had no idea where the company he founded would one day go. The firm that Earl Wyman and Sam Pickard acquired in 1934 has now become much more than a manufacturer of bib overalls.

The example set by Earl Wyman and the leadership characteristics he displayed were crucial to the company's growth beyond the American farmer and railroad man. Still, Fritz Hyde and Tom Wyman would be the first to remind people that literally thousands of employees in this country, and now around the world, have contributed in meaningful ways to the company's long-term success. They all helped to make OshKosh B'Gosh one of the most recognized brand names in American clothing history.

The corporate culture that Earl Wyman managed to cultivate as a young executive was passed along to his heirs, and they, in turn, bequeathed it to their heirs. Today those who have shared in the company's history sense that being a part of all this has been — and still is — something very special, and those who are leading OshKosh B'Gosh into its centennial celebration and beyond hold dear to their hearts the commitment to a philosophy, a colorful history and all of those common threads that have become a part of this American dream.

OSHKOSH B'GOSH
100
Celebrating A Century As The Genuine Article

1895

The Grove Manufacturing Company is incorporated on July 13 in Oshkosh, Wisconsin by Frank E. Grove, James G. Clark, J. Howard Jenkins and George M. Jones as a public company with a small number of closely held shares. Its business is making hickory-striped denim bib overalls for railroad workers and farmers. It begins operations with 10 employees.

1896

The company's name changes to the Oshkosh Clothing Manufacturing Company on December 22. Grove subsequently transfers control of the company to Jenkins and Clark.

1910

The company begins making child-size overalls as a novelty item for proud parents. Its early advertising slogan for the brand will be: "Work Clothes for Dad, Play Clothes for Sonny".

1911

William Pollock becomes company general manager and changes the name to Oshkosh Overall Company on January 25. While on a buying trip to New York, Pollock hears the phrase "Oshkosh b'gosh" in a vaudeville skit. In the fall, the company adopts OshKosh B'Gosh as its garment brand name, replacing J & C (Jenkins & Clark). The company is the first overall manufacturer to use 8-ounce denim in its garments. Oshkosh Overall Company employs 24 people.

1923

The company's line of garments now includes workwear pants, shirts and jackets in addition to adult and child-size overalls. It employs 265 people.

1924

The company introduces the first Vestbak® overalls.

1934

Earl Wyman and associates acquire a controlling interest in the company. William Pollock retires. Earl Wyman becomes chief executive officer.

1935

The company takes its first step toward national distribution, sponsoring regular broadcasts on a far-reaching Chicago radio station. The company has 450 employees.

1937

In February, OshKosh B'Gosh, Inc. becomes the company's official name.

1953

OshKosh B'Gosh employs 500 people and records sales of $5.5 million.

1954

To keep pace with growing consumer demand, OshKosh B'Gosh builds a second manufacturing plant, this one in Celina, Tennessee. The company is the first workwear manufacturer to use "grippers" (metal snap fasteners) in its garments.

1962

Miles Kimball Co., a mail order firm based in Oshkosh, features OshKosh B'Gosh children's overalls in its national catalog.

1963

Charles F. Hyde becomes president of OshKosh B'Gosh.

1964

OshKosh B'Gosh expands its manufacturing base, opening its third plant, this one in Columbia, Kentucky, and hits $6.9 million in sales.

1966

Charles F. Hyde succeeds his father-in-law, Earl Wyman, as chief executive officer of OshKosh B'Gosh.

1975

OshKosh B'Gosh records $24.8 million in sales.

1978

Bloomingdales and Saks Fifth Avenue order OshKosh B'Gosh children's overalls for sale in their stores. Other retailers follow suit. Retailers ask for more styles

1979

Children's apparel comprises 15 percent of OshKosh B'Gosh annual sales. The company adds two more manufacturing plants, the start of a growth spurt in production capacity.

1980

OshKosh B'Gosh starts making infant wear.

1981

OshKosh opens its first outlet store in West Bend, Wisconsin.

OshKosh opens its first regional sales office in New York City.

1984

OshKosh B'Gosh hits $100 million in sales.

1985

OshKosh B'Gosh stock is listed on the NASDAQ exchange under the symbol GOSHA.

1986

The company launches its first Picture Perfect Photo Contest, asking parents and other relatives to send in photos of children in OshKosh B'Gosh clothes. It anticipates 50,000 entries; it receives more than 130,000. OshKosh B'Gosh employs more than 3,300 people in Wisconsin, Kentucky and Tennessee.

1990

OshKosh B'Gosh establishes an international division to supervise sales of its children's apparel, men's wear and licensed products throughout the world and establishes OshKosh B'Gosh Europe, a wholly-owned subsidiary, to further establish a stronger presence in Europe.

OshKosh B'Gosh acquires Essex Outfitters, the U. S. children's licensee of Boston Trader Ltd., a strong brand in upscale children's wear covering sizes newborn through 20.

1991

OshKosh B'Gosh leases its first foreign manufacturing facility in Choloma, Honduras.

1992

Douglas W. Hyde succeeds his father, Charles, as chief executive officer of OshKosh B'Gosh.

1993

Children's clothing comprises 95 percent of the company's annual sales. The company introduces a children's wear direct mail catalog.

OshKosh B'Gosh ranks sixth in the national EquiTrend Survey, which gauges the strength of brand names by measuring consumers' perception of brand quality.

1994

OshKosh B'Gosh opens its first two showcase retail stores for children's wear and accessories in London and Paris in March and a third on Fifth Avenue in New York City in November. The company now operates five stores in Europe (two retail stores and three outlet stores), and 60 outlet stores in the United States.

Apparel Industry magazine honors OshKosh B'Gosh with the 1994 Gold Star Award for superior technology application, management and marketing.

The company's licensing agreement with Boston Trader Ltd. ends.

OshKosh B'Gosh introduces a line of upscale children's wear under the brand name Genuine Kids.

OshKosh B'Gosh clothing is sold in over 70 countries around the world. The company empoys 5,967 people.

59

Acknowledgements

Though I have known the name virtually all my life, the illustrious history of perhaps the grandest brand name in apparel around the world is something only now I've enjoyed the privilege of learning first hand and sharing with you.

Wonderful people make wonderful things and so true that is of the people who are and have been so important to the OshKosh B'Gosh story.

Naturally, I must thank the Hyde and Wyman families for their time and precious recollections. They are the first to admit that without the loyal colleagues they worked with over the years, quite simply the OshKosh B'Gosh name would have far less meaning. Meeting many of them through the process of putting this history to pen is something not soon to be forgotten.

A special thanks to Anne Spangler, who, among many other things also serves the company as the corporate librarian. She helped navigate through all the memories and written documents which have been carefully preserved and cataloged. Though she may not realize it, she and others before her played a dynamic role in allowing this all to take shape.

My granddad, Bill Chesnut wore OshKosh B'Gosh overalls and at the same time taught me the value of keeping good stories not to oneself but to be shared. In that, I must finally also thank John C. Behrens who without his guidance and care not a stitch of this great story would have been sewn by me.

Jim Naleid

INDEX

*Bold listings refer to illustrated
material.*